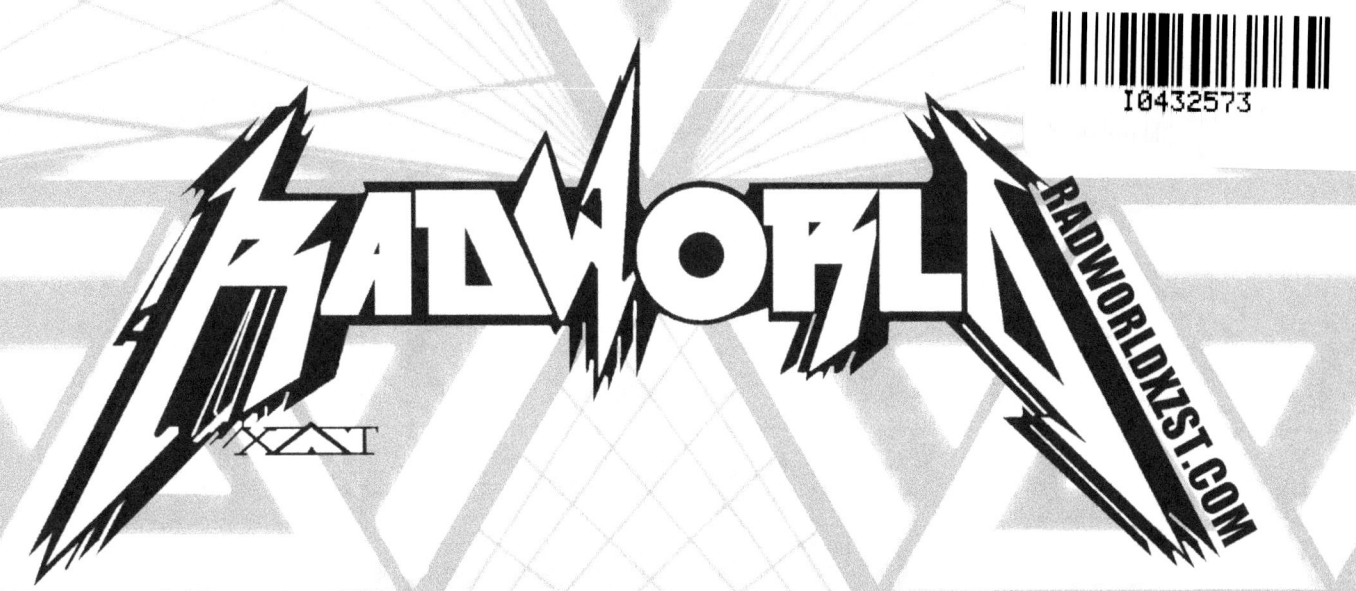

RADWORLDXZST COLORING BOOK
THE COLORING BOOK FOR EVERYONE
ARTISTIC STRATEGIC DESIGN BY TONEXZST

THE COLORING BOOK II

2017

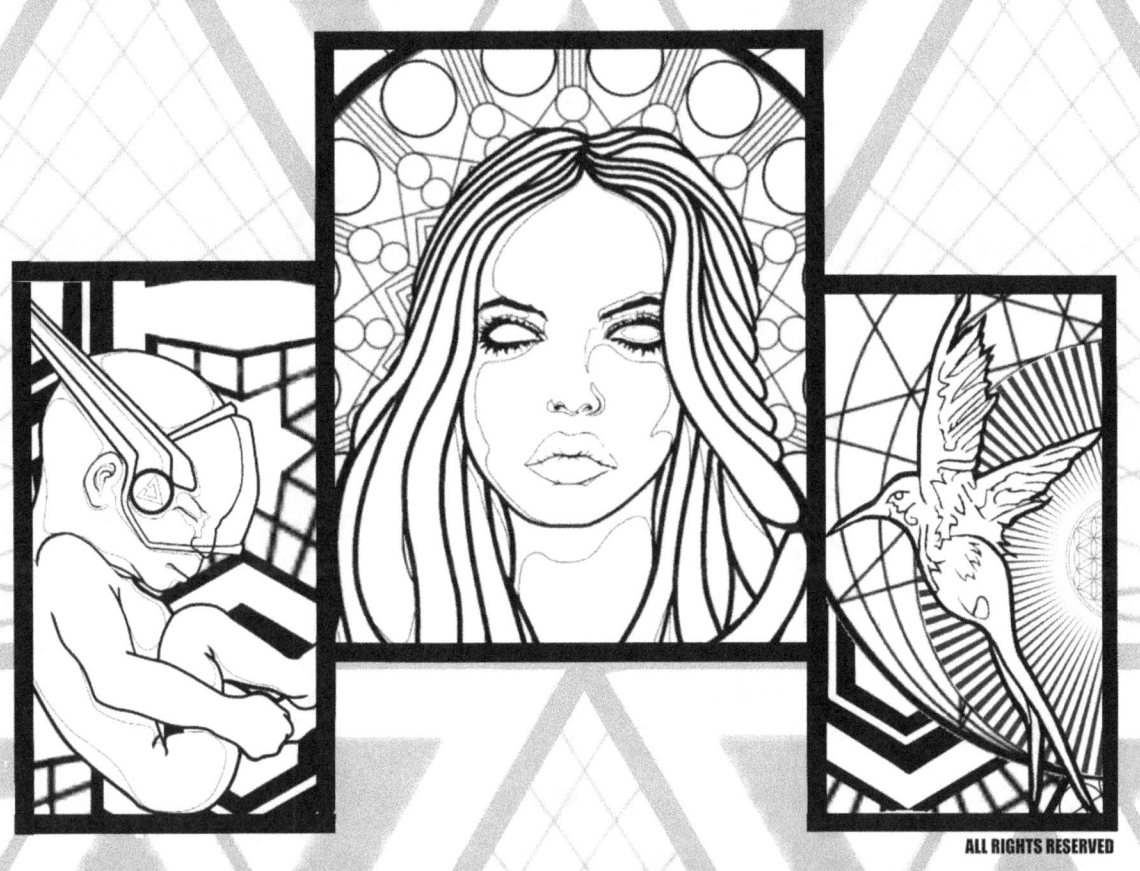

ALL RIGHTS RESERVED

SKRIBBLE TEST PAGE

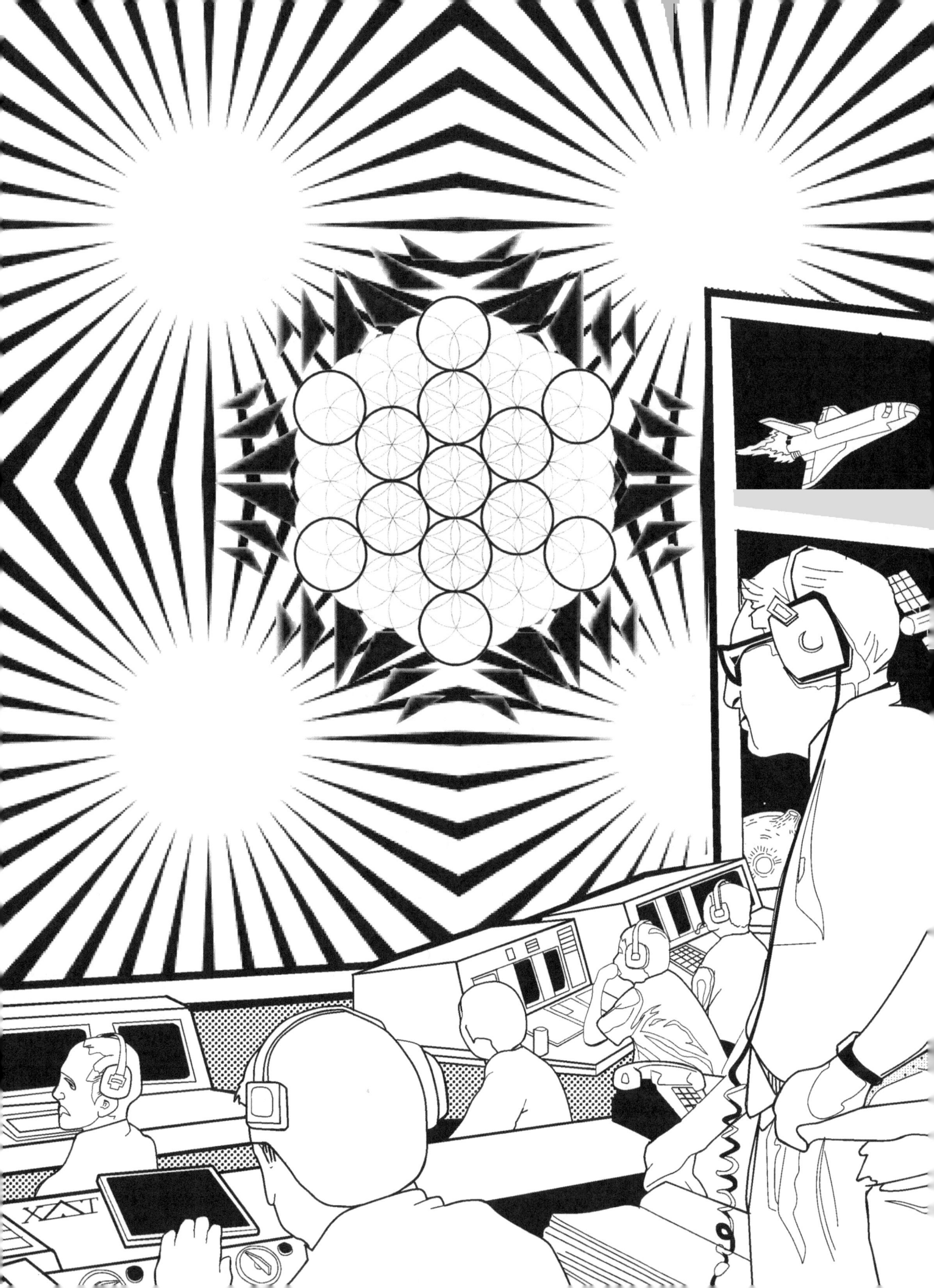

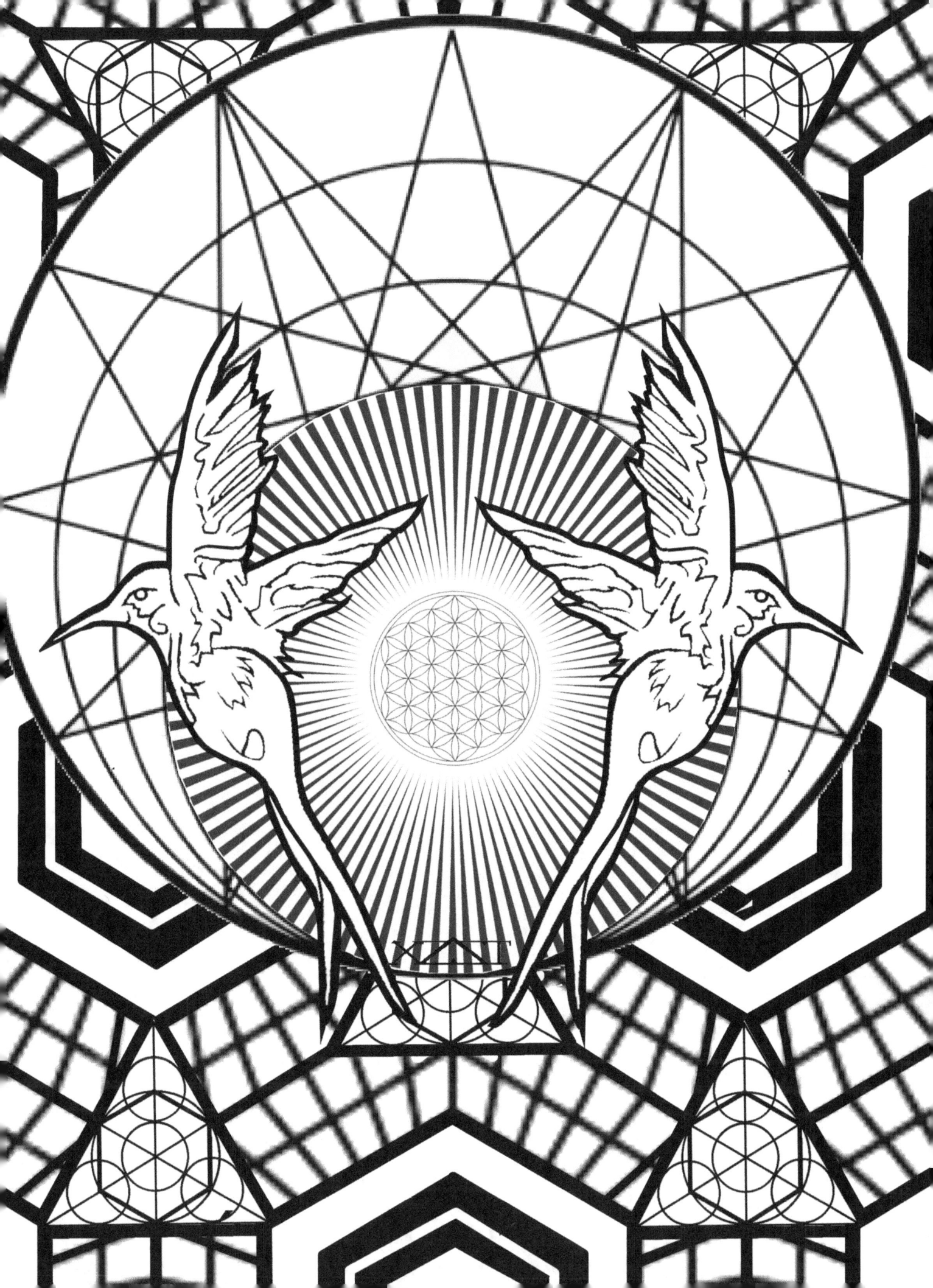

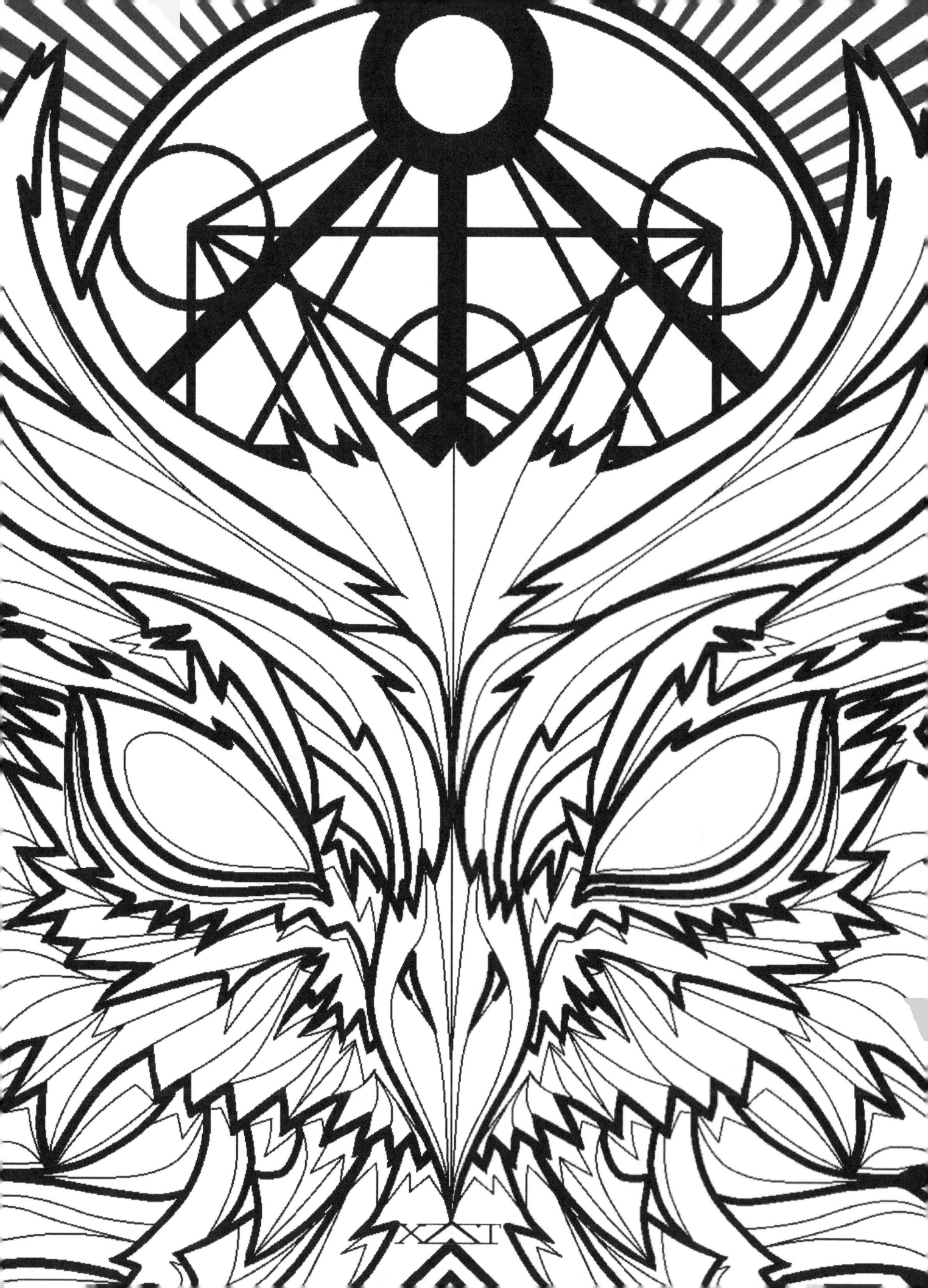

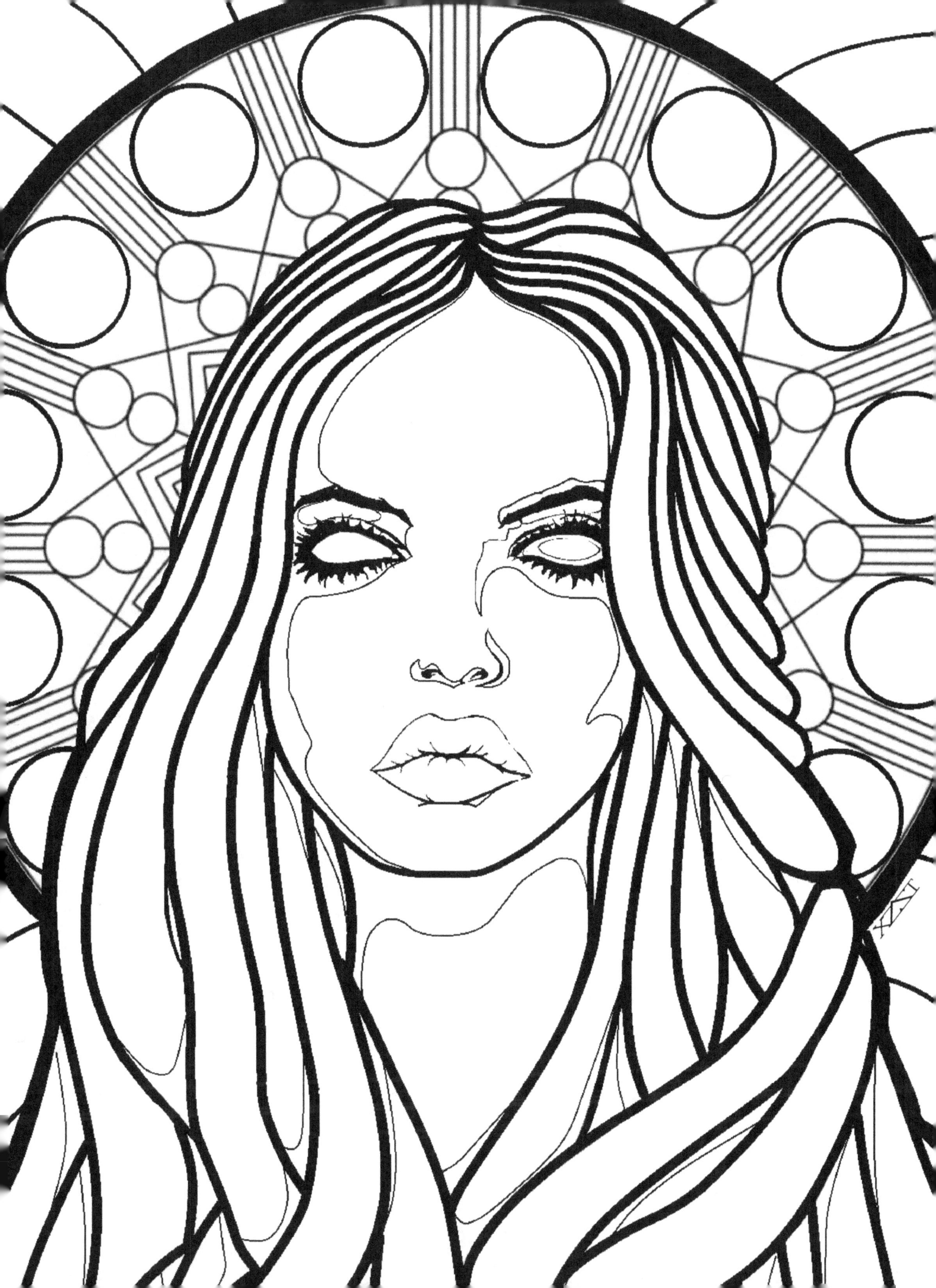

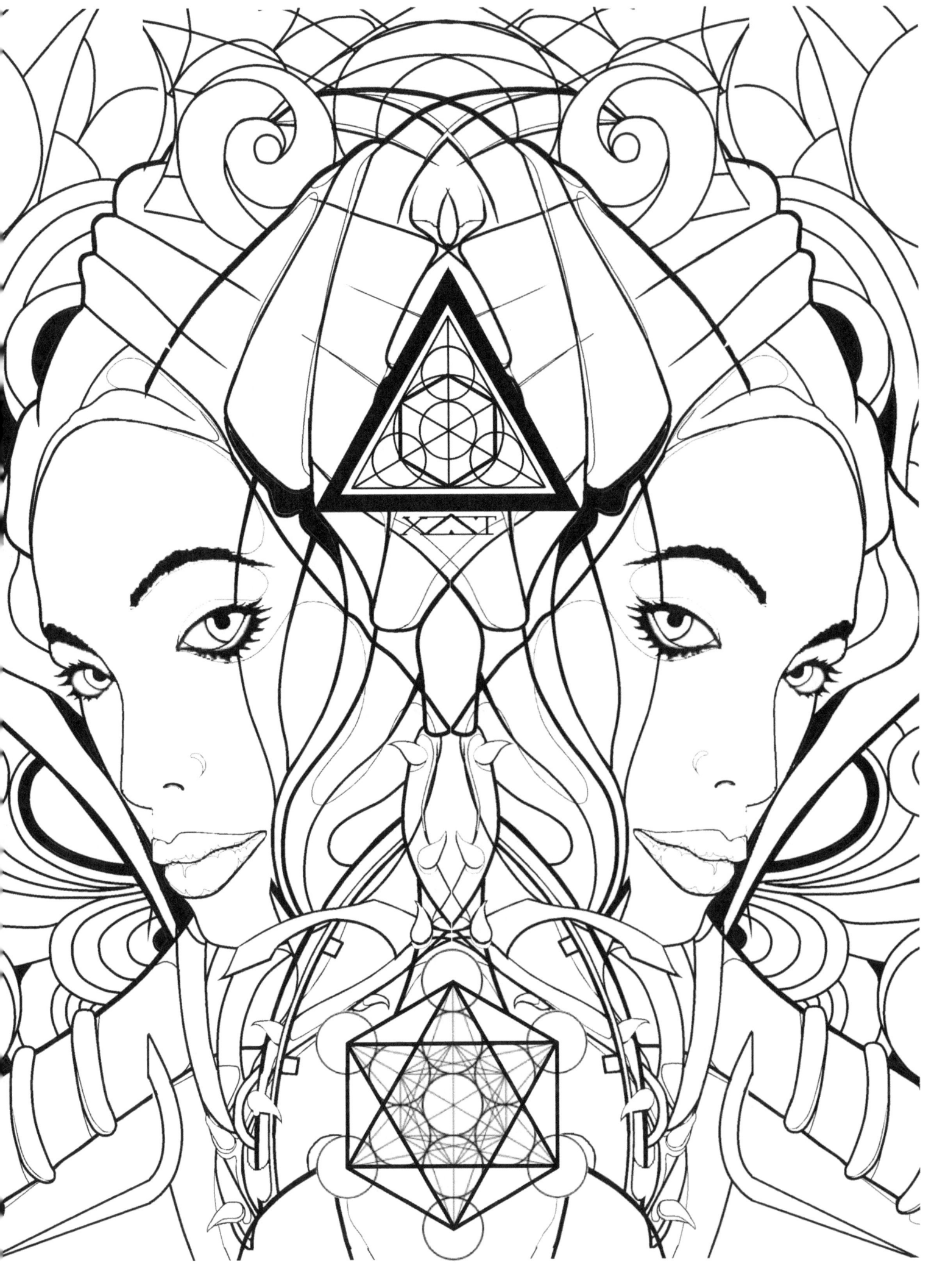

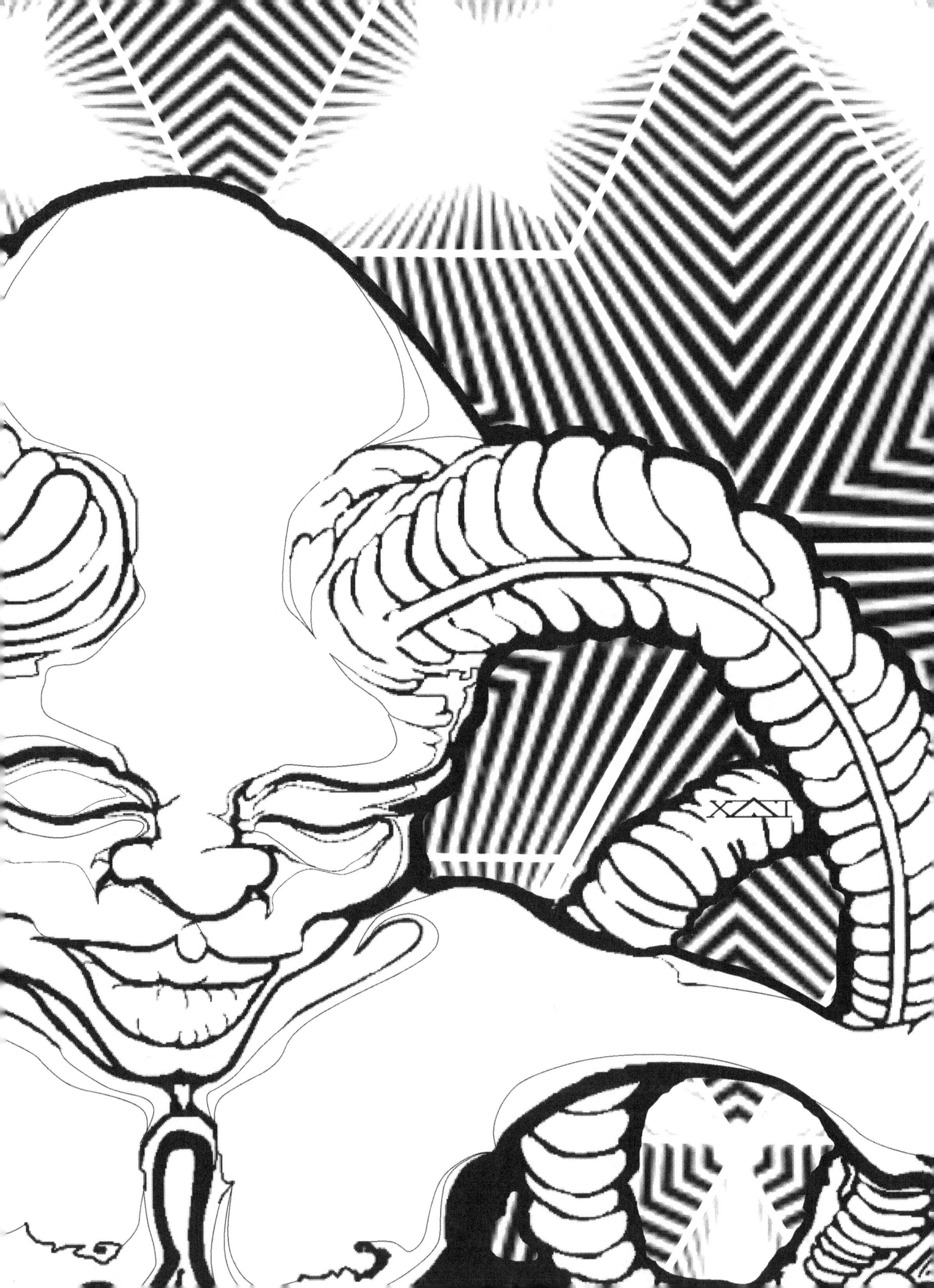

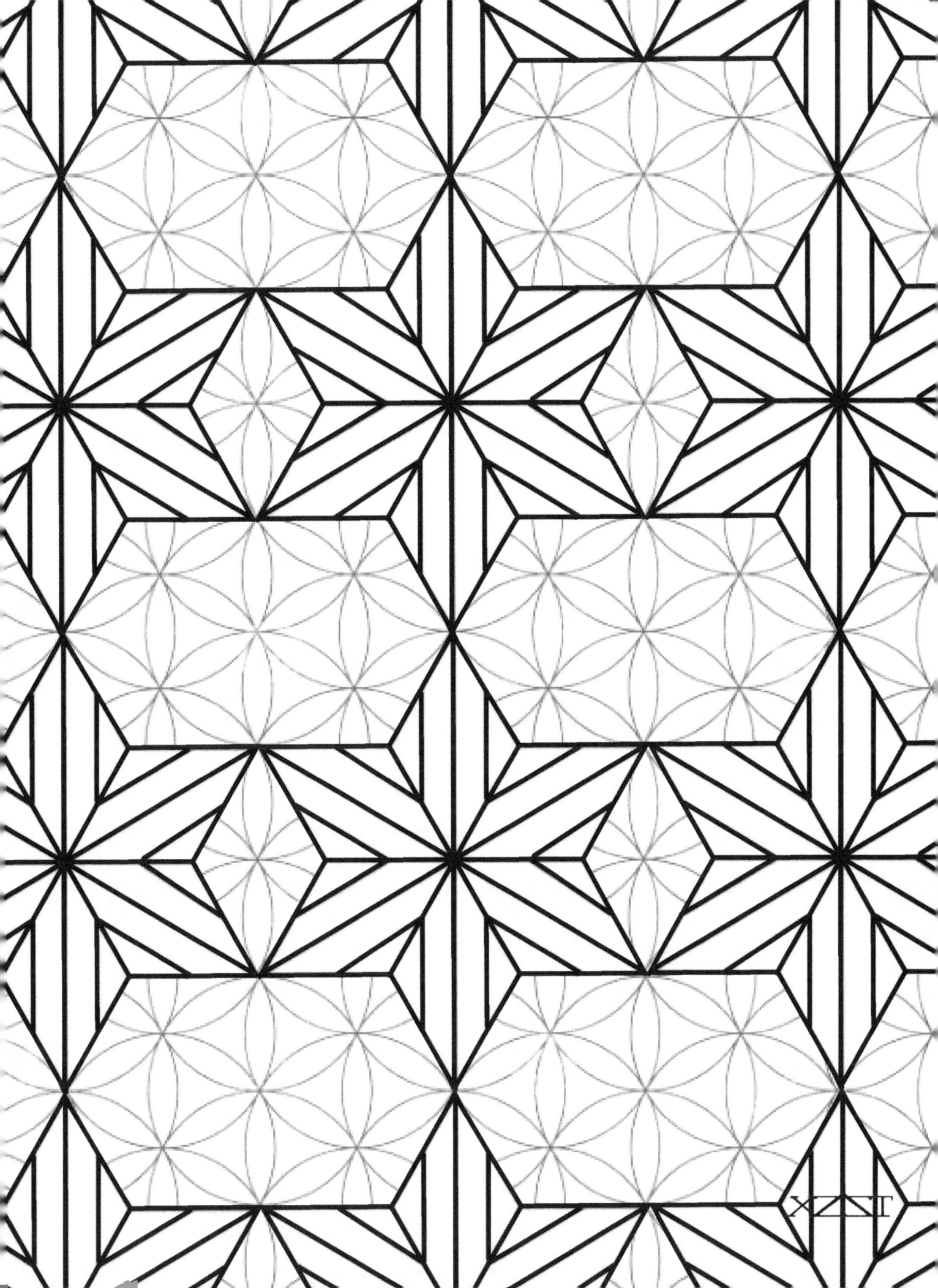

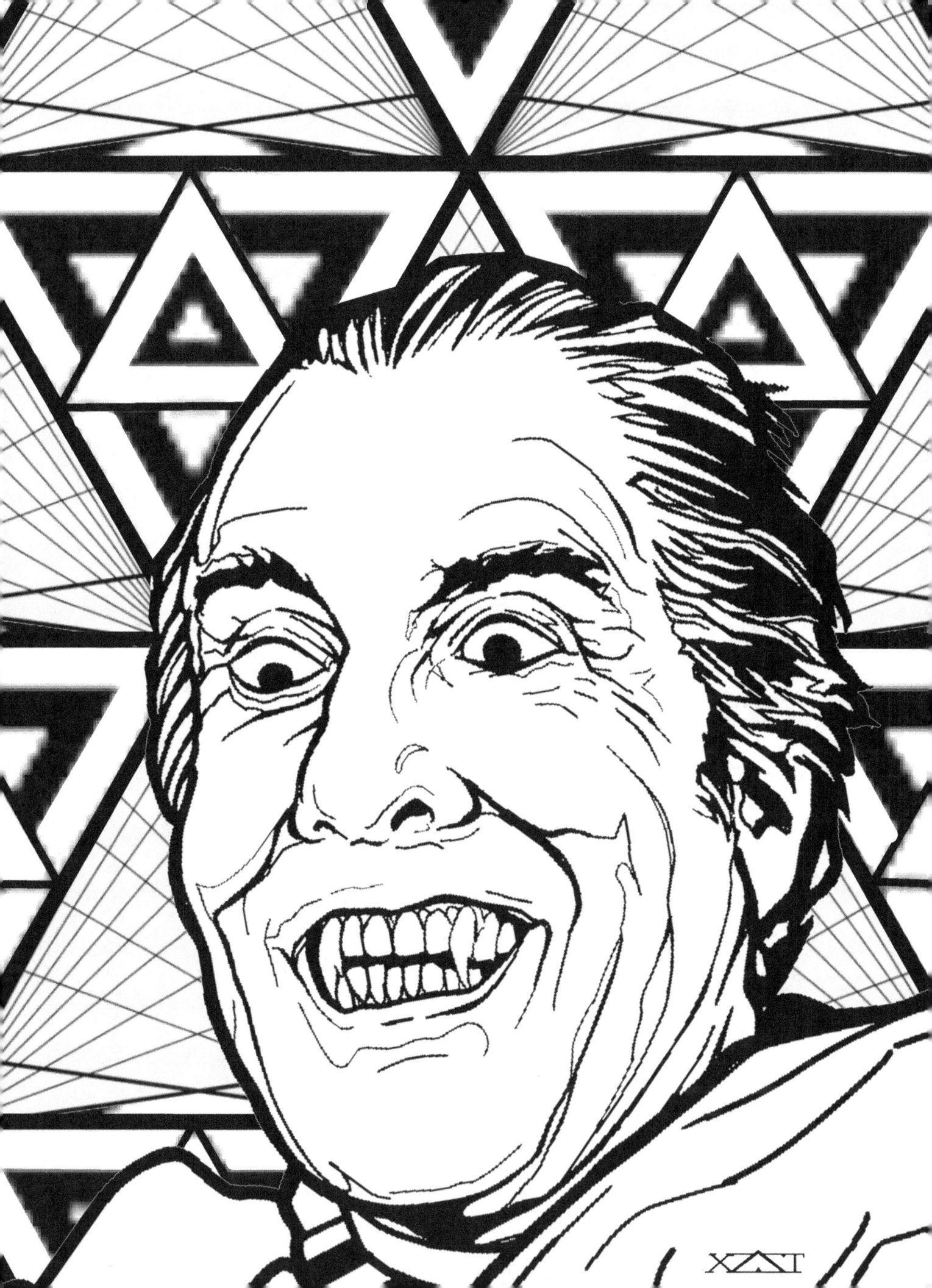

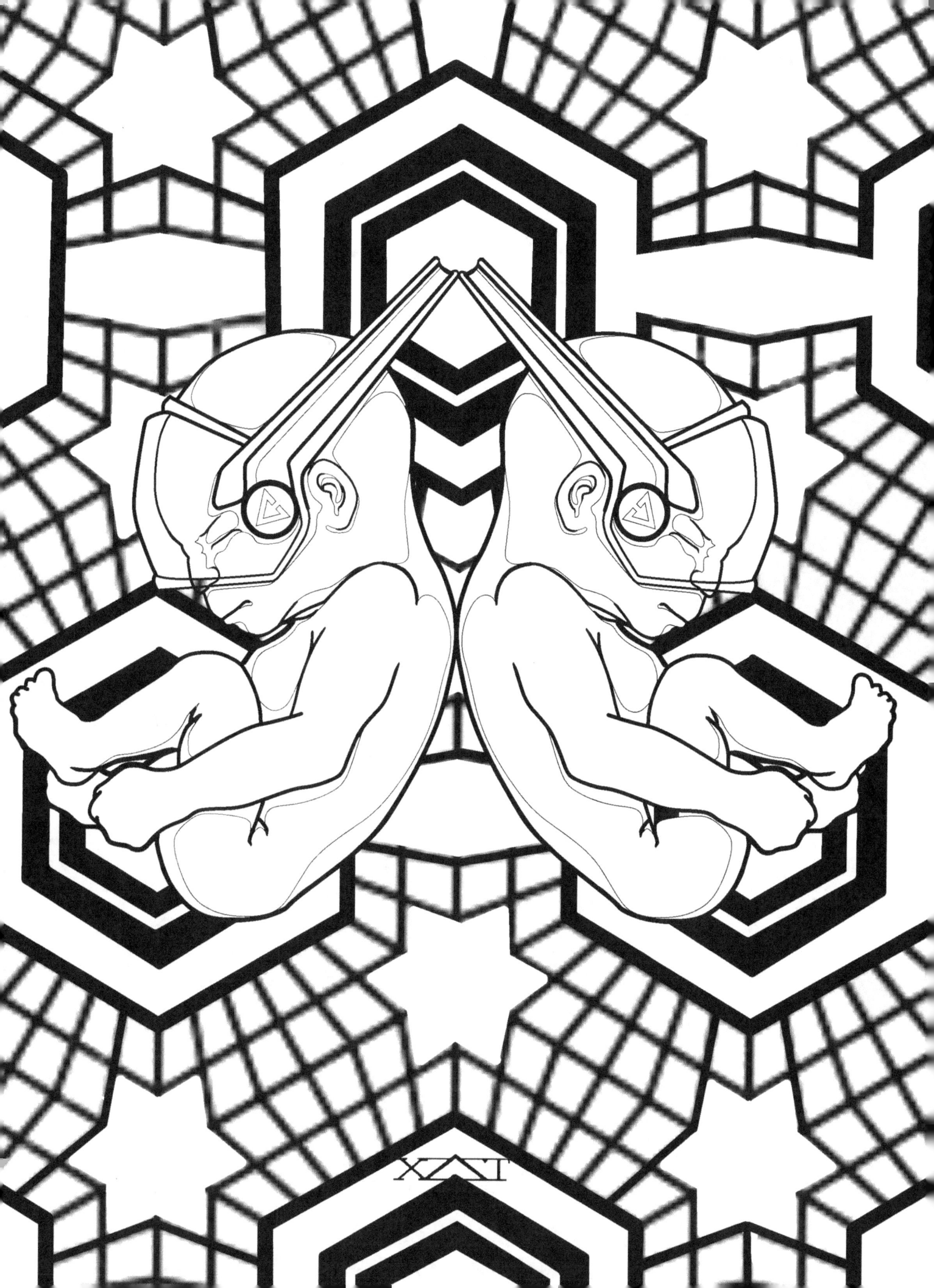

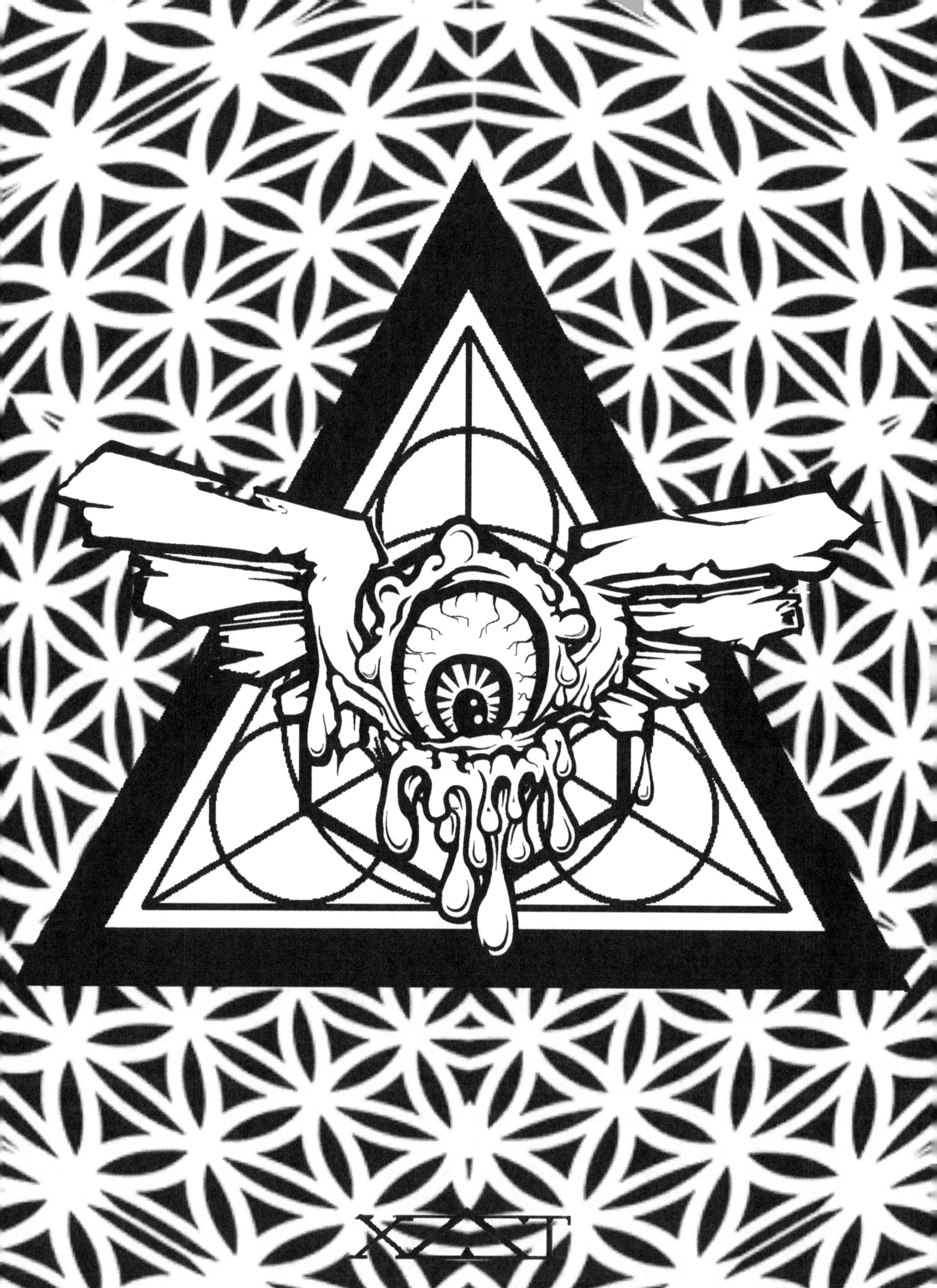

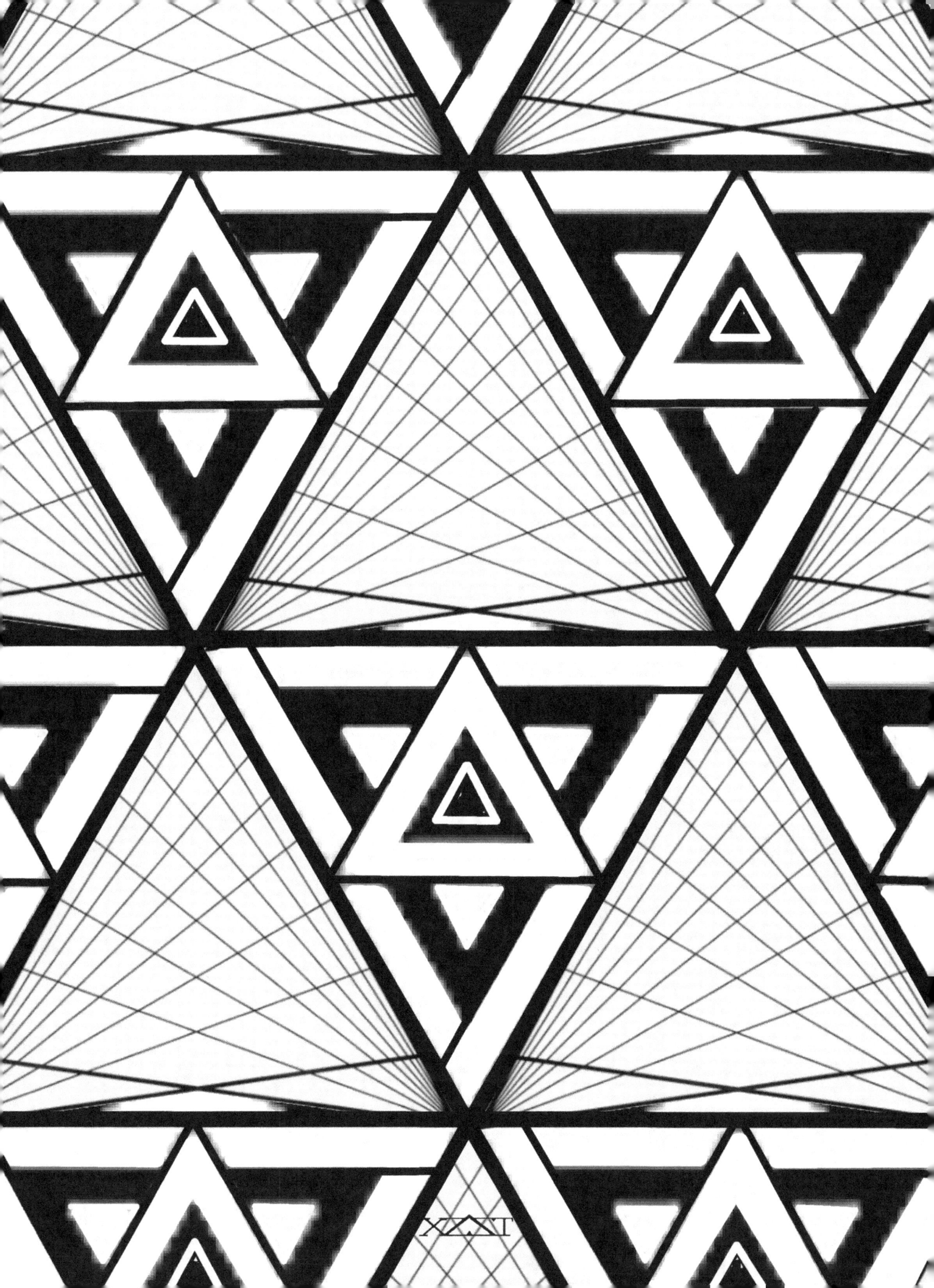

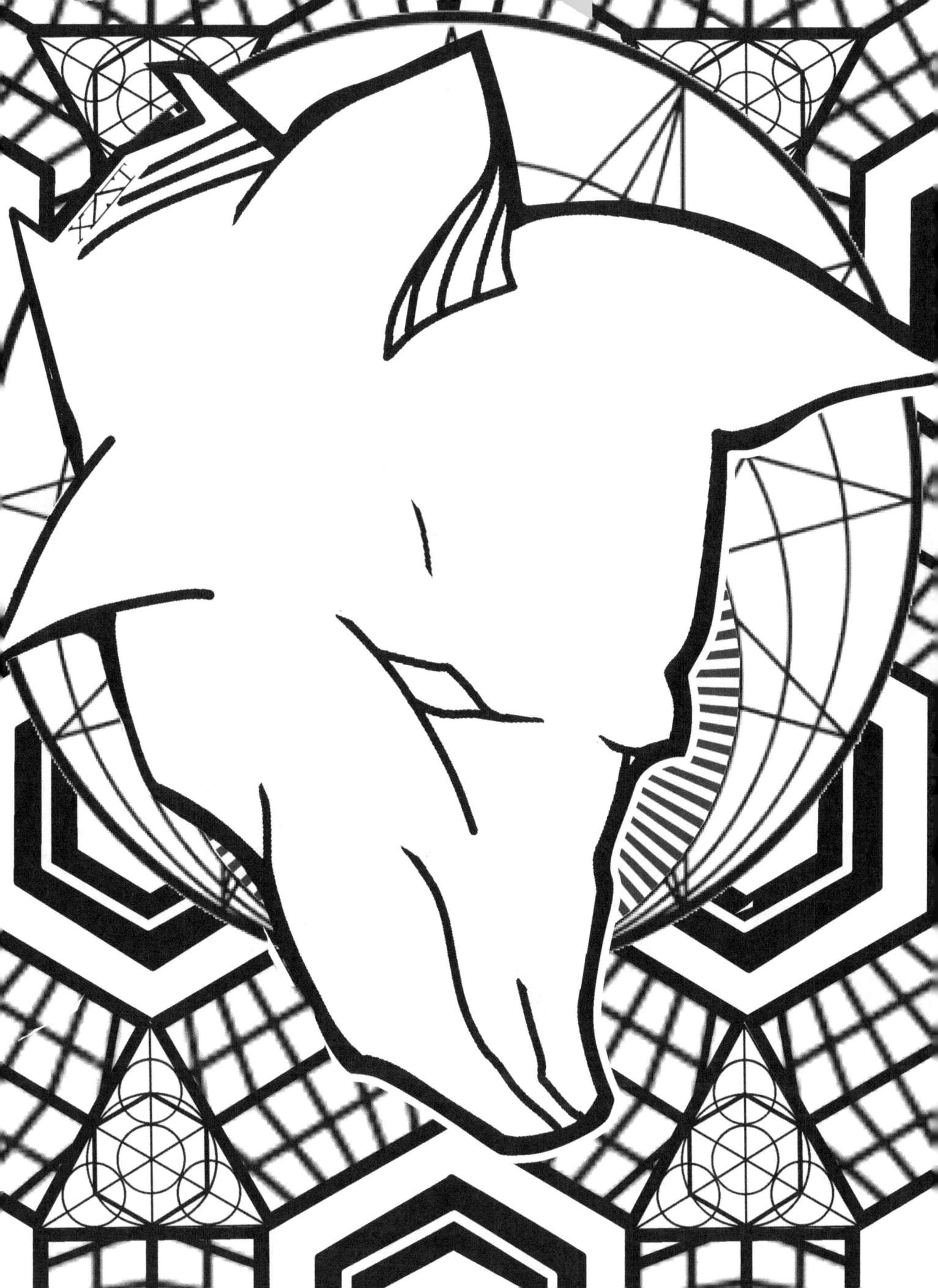

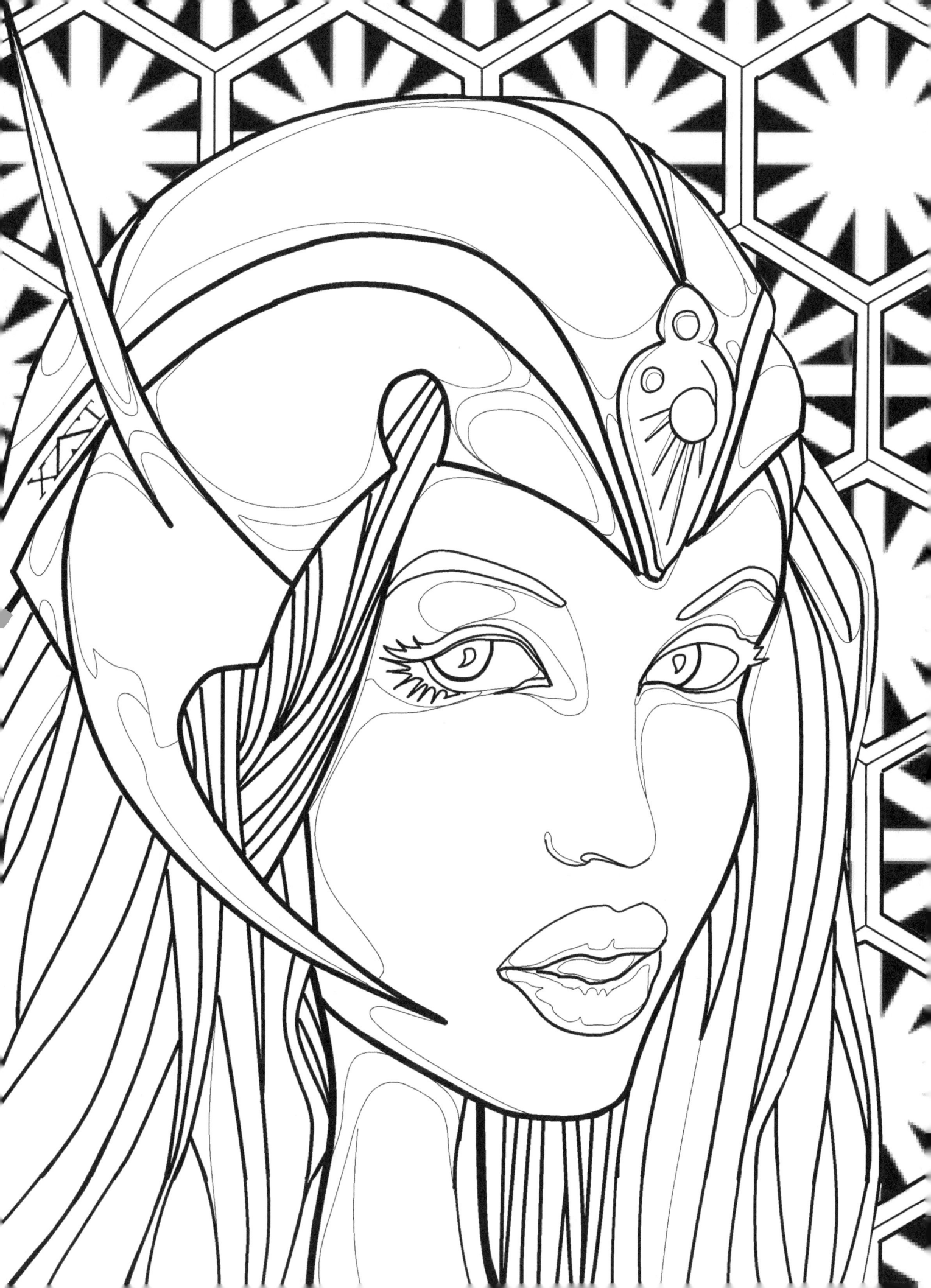

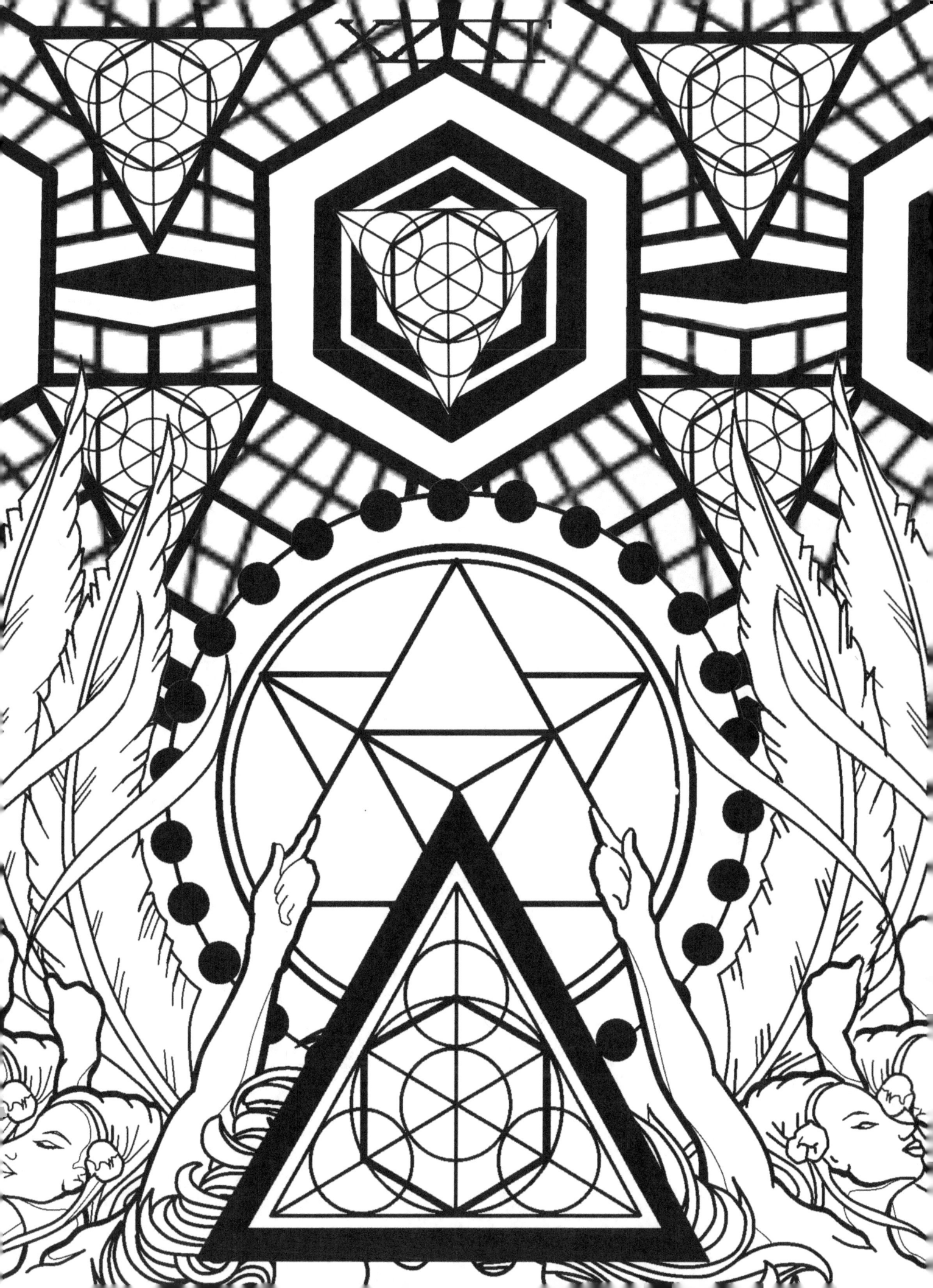

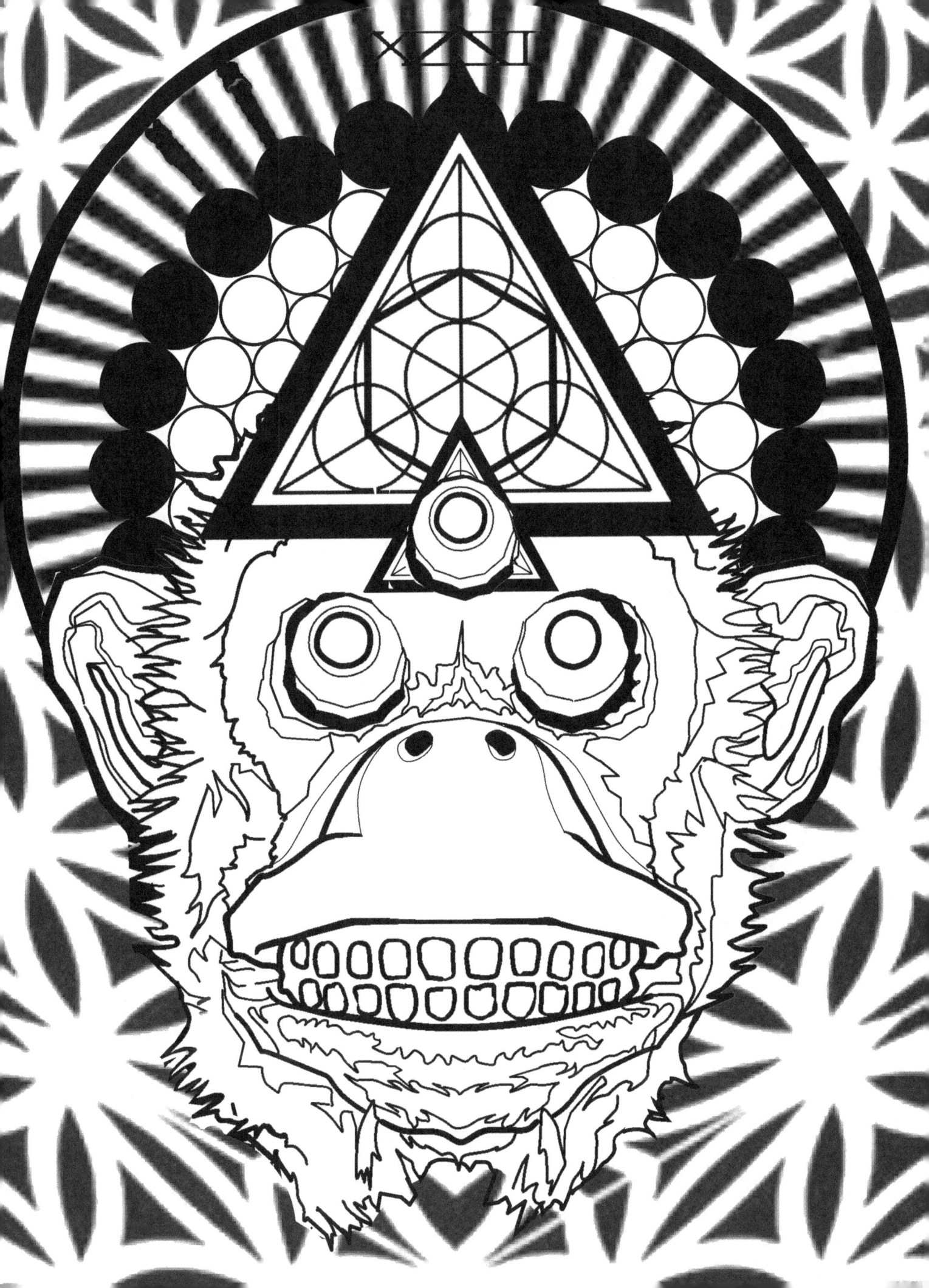

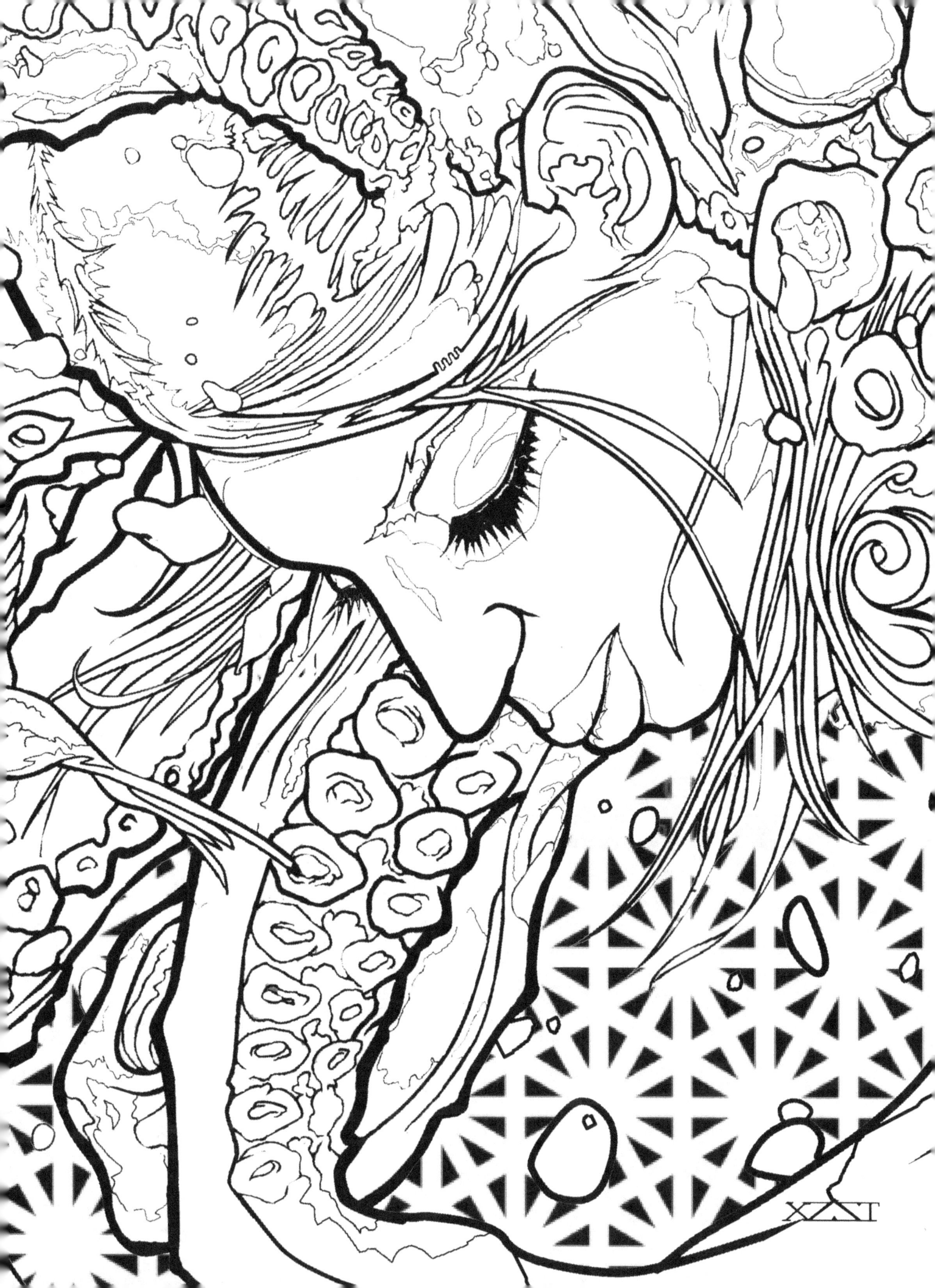

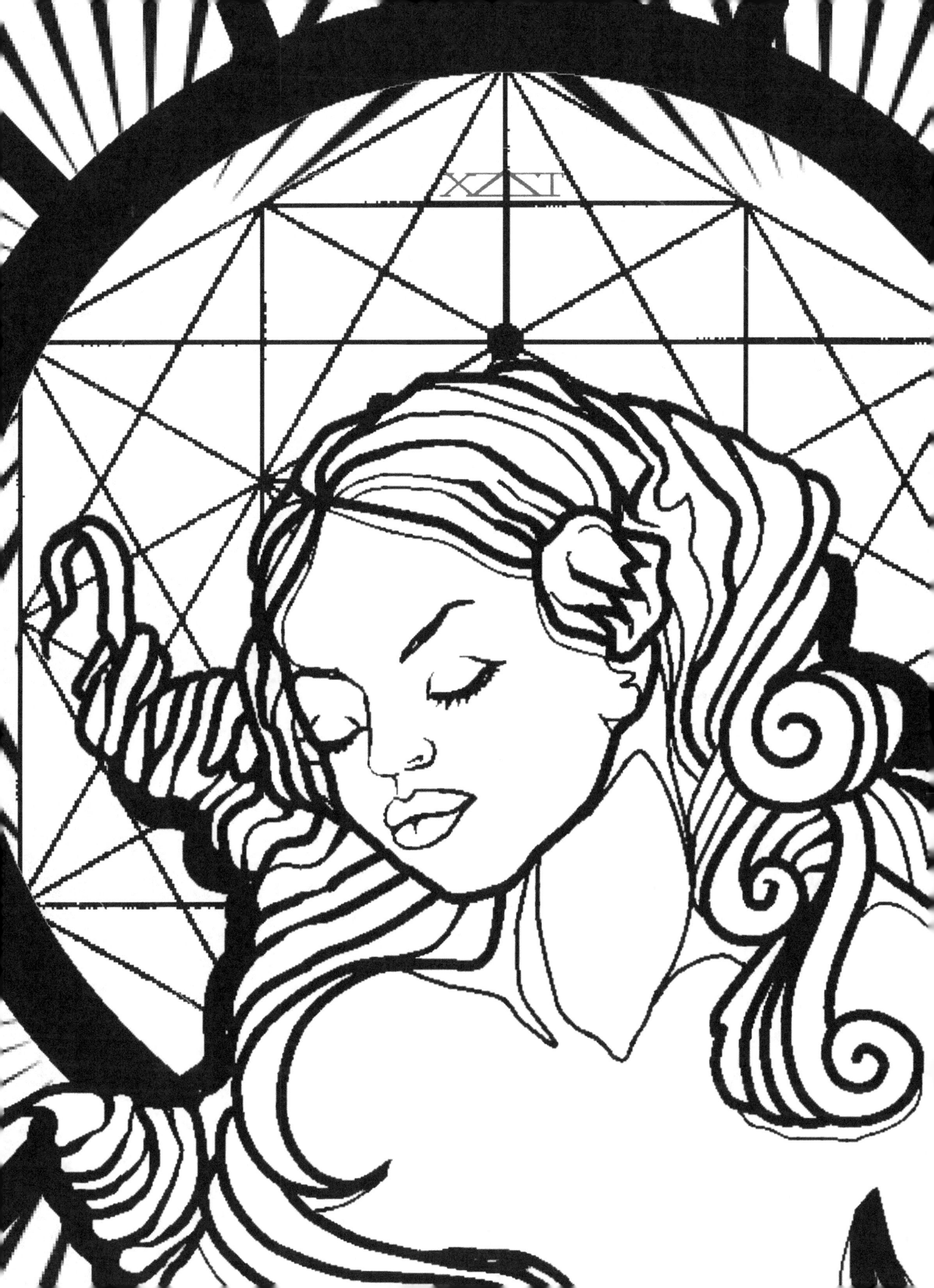

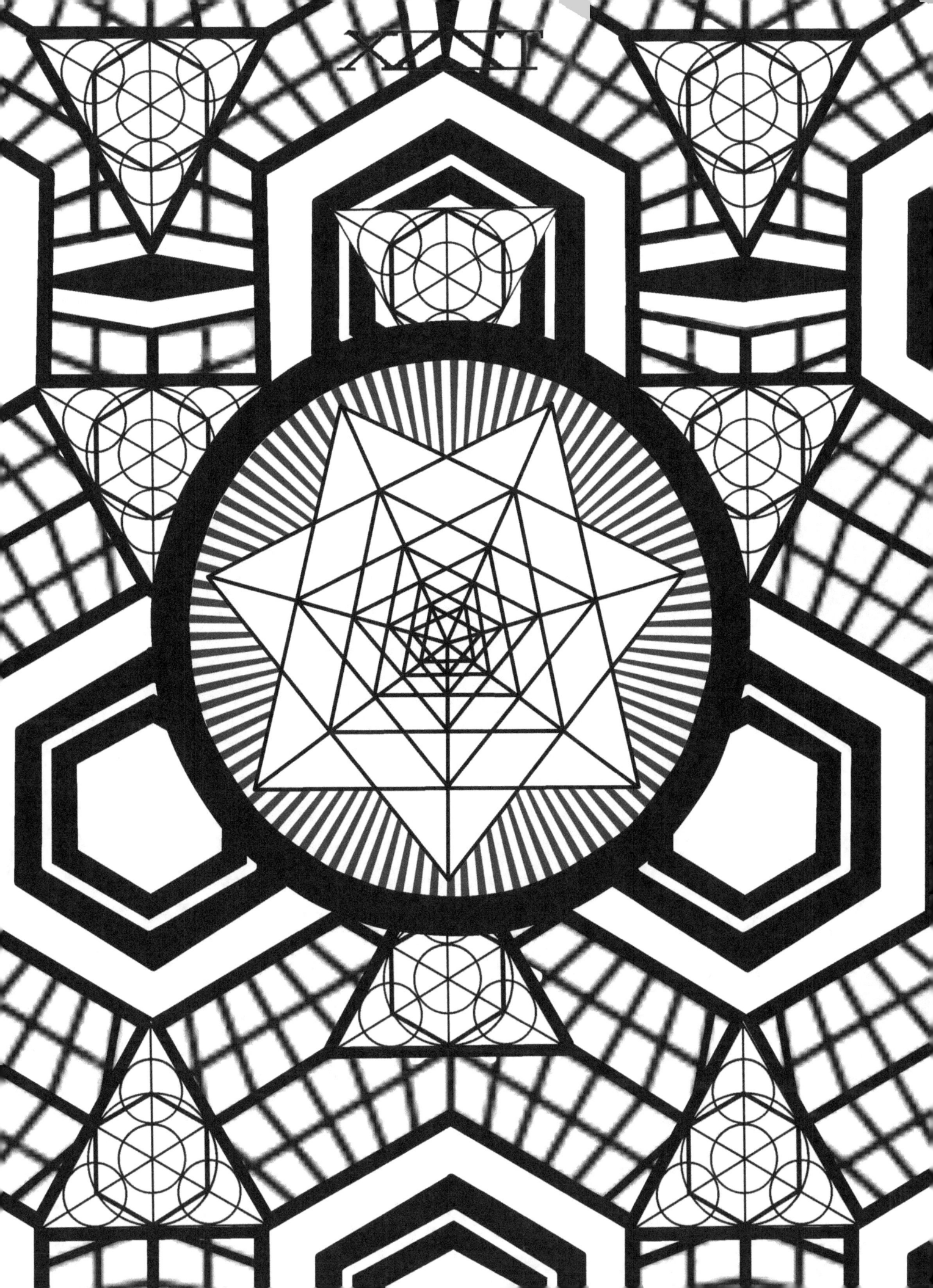

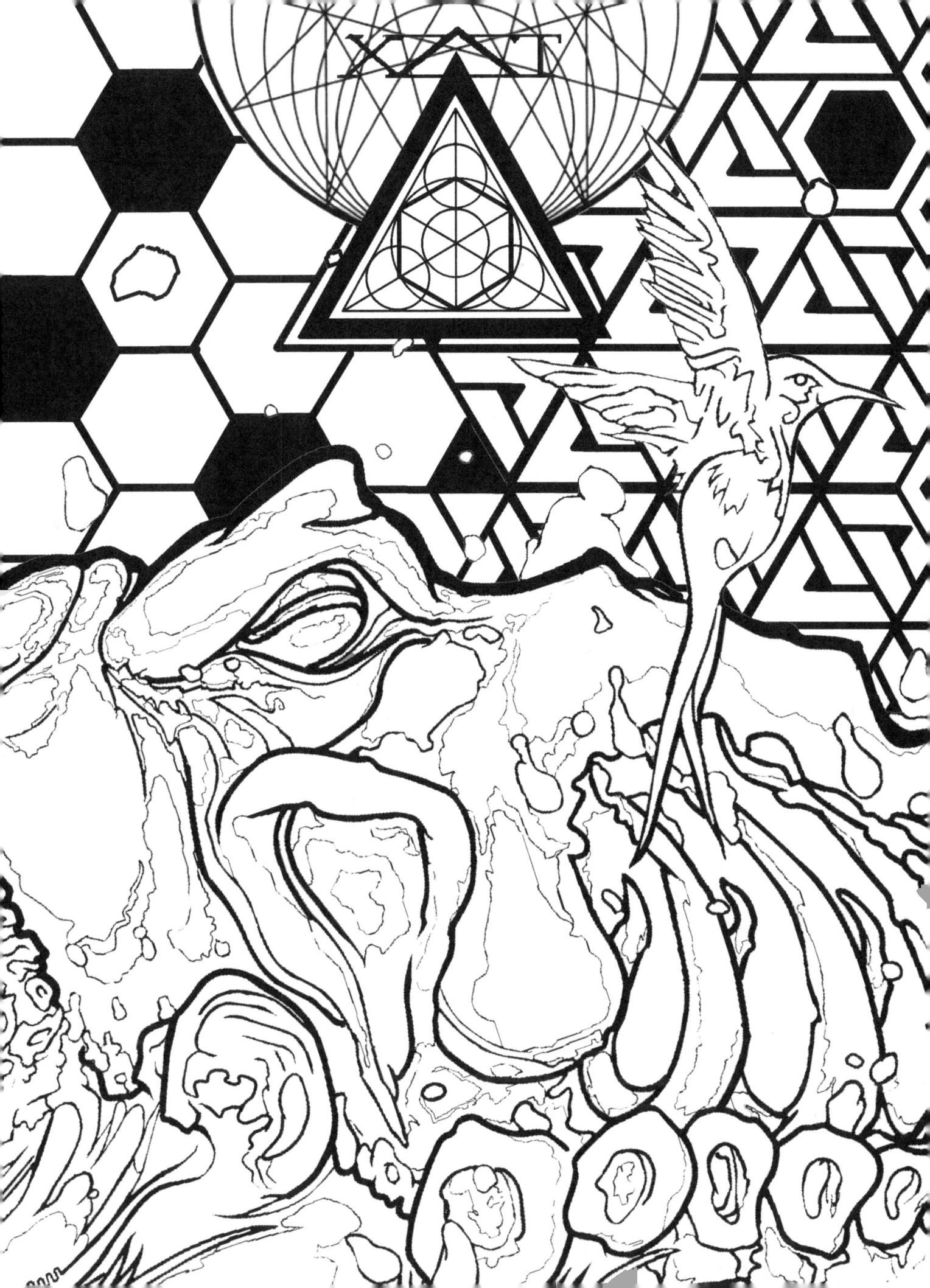

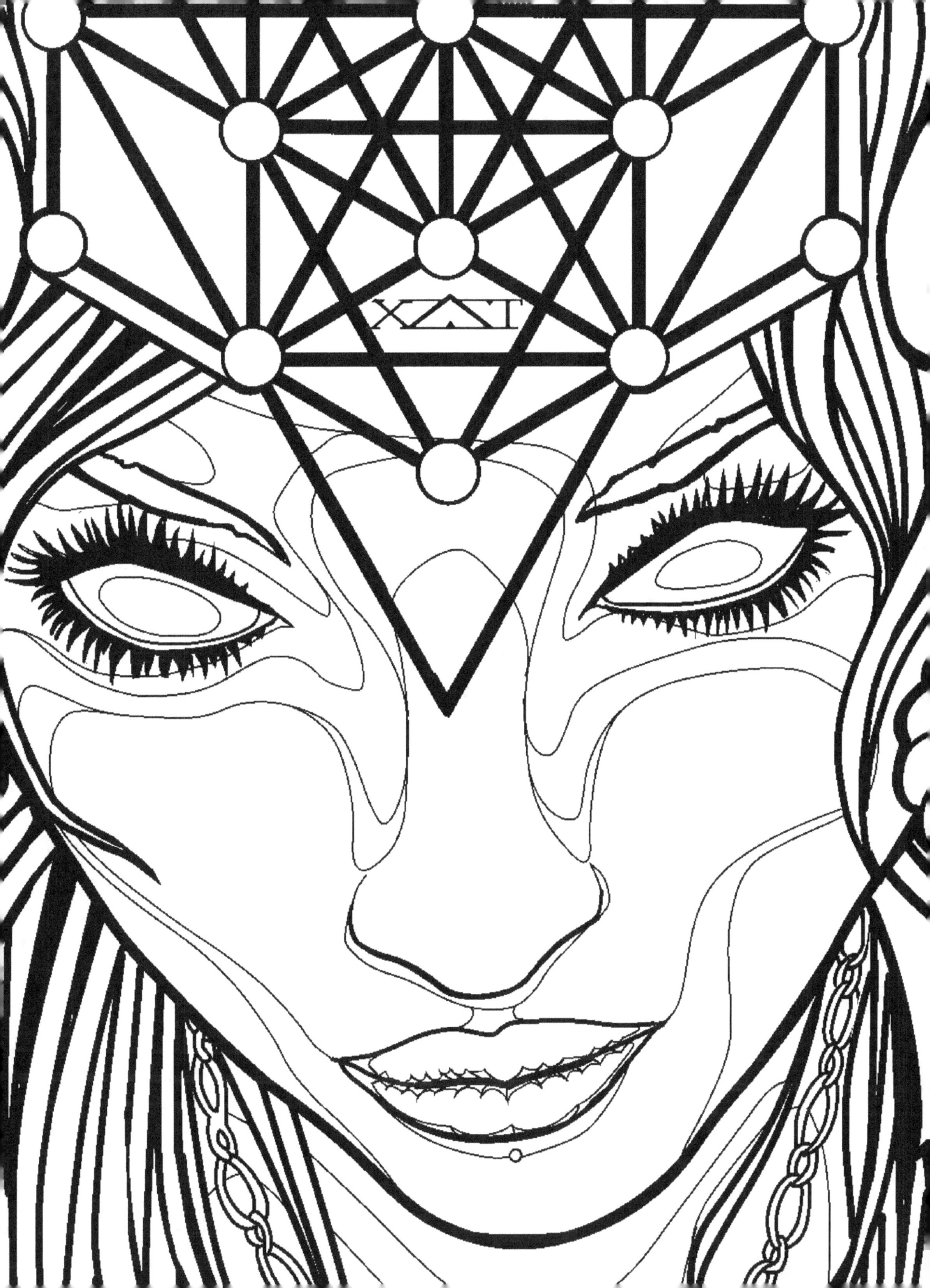

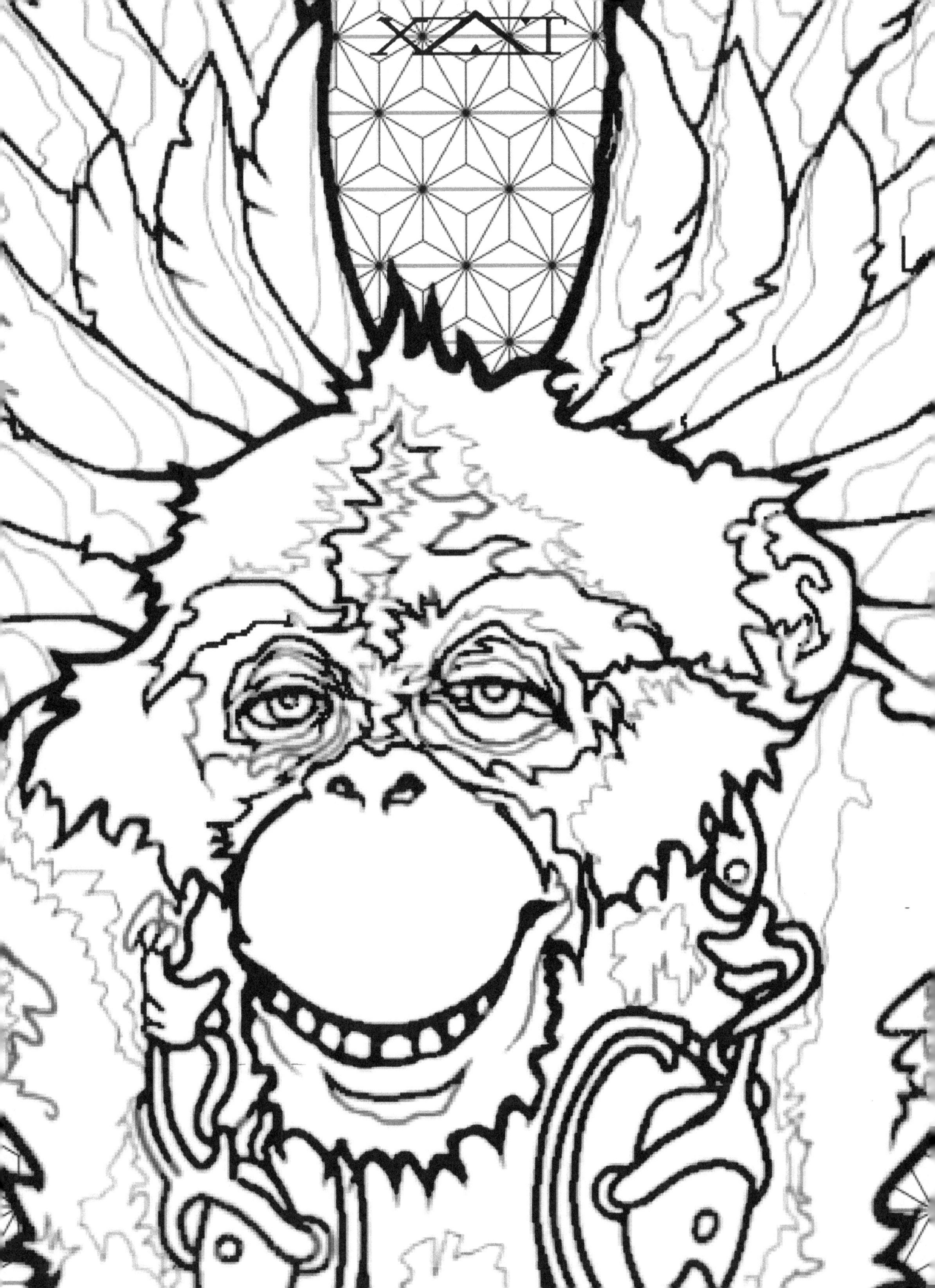

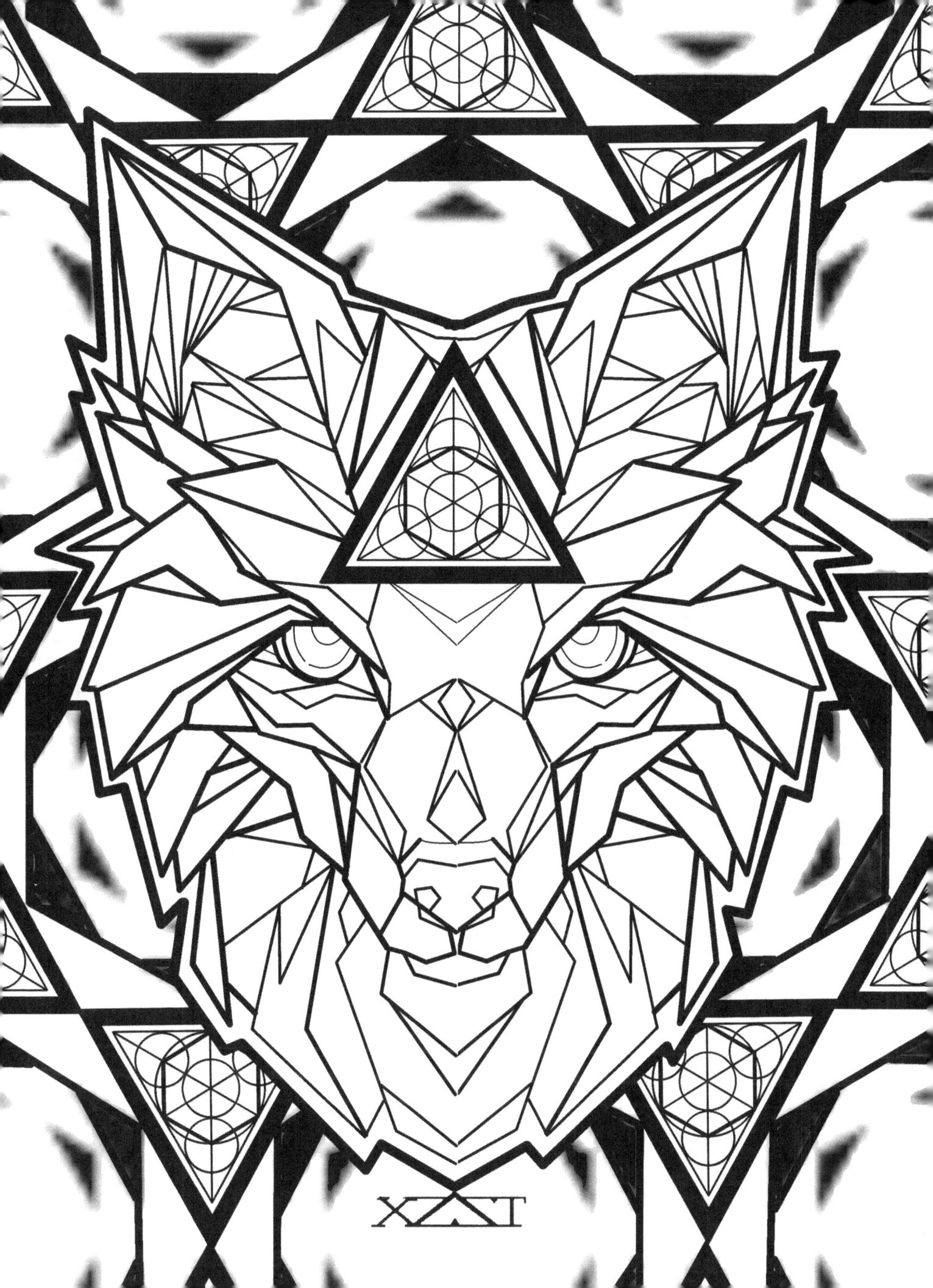

SKRIBBLE TEST PAGE

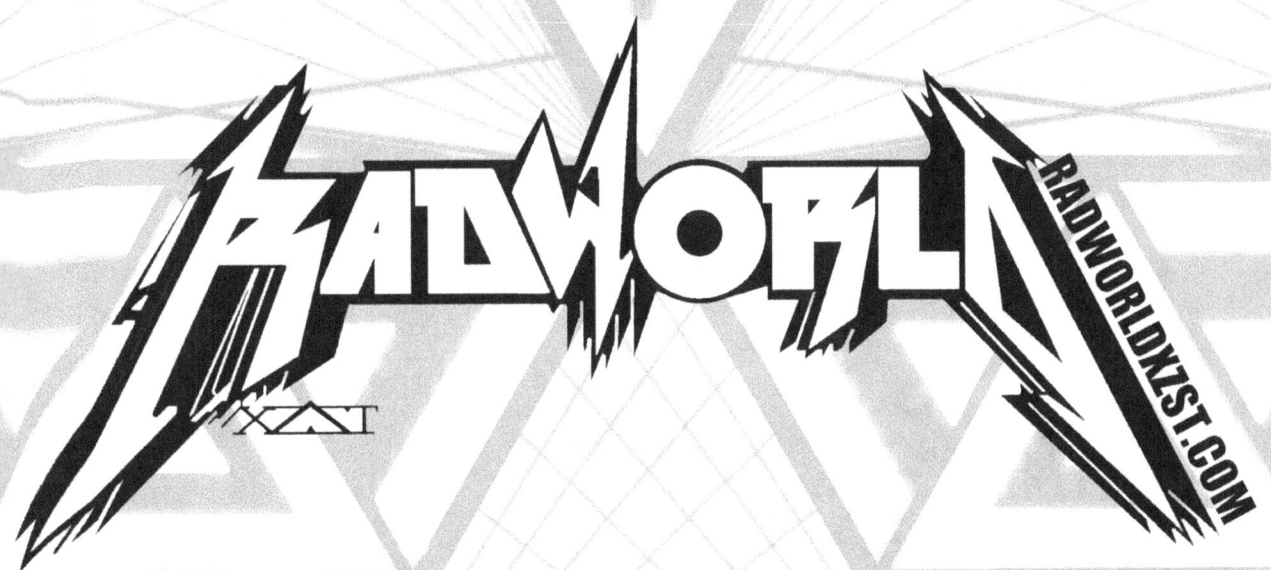

RADWORLDXZST COLORING BOOK
THE COLORING BOOK FOR EVERYONE
ARTISTIC STRATEGIC DESIGN BY TONEXZST

THE COLORING BOOK II
2017

I WOULD LIKE TO GIVE THANKS TO THOSE WHO MADE IT THROUGH THE QUEST OF THESE PAGES. I HOPE THAT THE TIME SPENT INSIDE THE PAGES OF THIS COLORING BOOK GAVE YOU RELAXATION, MEDITATION, AND POSITIVE EXPERIENCES.
TONEXZST 2017
ALL RIGHTS FOR THE ART IN THIS BOOK IS OWNED BY THE ARTIST. IF YOU ARE INTERESTED IN USING ANY OF THE ART FOR PROMOTIONS, PLEASE CONTACT ME AT
RADWORLDXZST@GMAIL.COM

ORDER MORE AT RADWORLDXZST.COM

ALL RIGHTS RESERVED

www.ingramcontent.com/pod-product-compliance
Lightning Source LLC
Chambersburg PA
CBHW081122240526
45470CB00019B/2906